YOUR SIMPLE PATH TO WEALTH

The Ultimate Guide To Build Your Financial Freedom And Significant Improvement Of Your Life

INTRODUCTION

Have you ever thought of how your life would be if money wasn't an issue...

....where money was not a determining factor of almost every decision you make in life?

Would you be working at the job you are in right now? Would you live where you stay currently? Would you drive the car that you are driving today? And would you spend your time on the things that you spend your time on today?

The answer is probably no.

You would probably quit that job you hate so much and do what makes you happy, live in a town that makes you feel at home, and use your time on things that add value to your life. In short, you would live your best life.

What if I told you that could be a reality for you. That you can achieve financial freedom and money stops being a determinant of everything that you do?

Well, it really is possible. You can achieve financial freedom, and you don't even have to be a genius or a financial guru. You just need to read this guide and follow its instructions. Amazing ha!

What this guide is going to show you is a proven formula to financial freedom that is complete with clear and simple to follow action steps.

By reading this book, you will get to understand what financial freedom is, why financial freedom is rare, why it's important for you, and how you can actually achieve it.

Let's get to it.

TABLE OF CONTENTS

WHAT IS FINANCIAL FREEDOM?

You now must be eager to learn the secret to financial freedom.

That is great.

But before you can get to know that, you need to first understand what financial freedom really is. Besides, how can you even reach a goal (financial freedom) that you don't understand in the first place?

What Is Financial Freedom?

As you saw earlier, financial freedom enables you to make life decisions without having money in your mind, but what does it mean to be financially free? If you make it your goal, what are you really working towards?

If you ask around, you will notice that different people have different definitions of what financial freedom is. Some will tell you it is being able to buy anything that you want whenever you want it. Others will tell you it is being rich and others will tell you it's living a life without debts. While there is some truth in all those definitions, they are all half-baked definitions when they stand on their own.

So what is the full definition?

It is the ability to have enough disposable (especially passive) income to cater for your living expenses.

As you can see, it is really not about being rich and having a lot of money, although that is a possibility and there is nothing wrong with that, but about you having an income (don't forget I mentioned that it would be best if it is passive) that can cover all your day to day expenses, including rent, gas, food, clothing, holidays, you name it - enabling you to spend your time doing the things that you love and care about instead of doing things for the sole purpose of making money.

Why Is Financial Freedom Important?

Financial freedom is important because achieving it comes with rewards that add quality to your life. These rewards help you go from a person you need to be to a person you want to be.

To demonstrate that and to show you just how beneficial financial freedom is, here are eight benefits of financial freedom.

1. *It allows you to uphold your values*

Have you ever worked in a job that asked you to do things that went against your values, but you did in anyway because you didn't want to lose your job?

A good example is you working at a hospital as a doctor and the institution has a policy where doctors can't conduct an emergency operation on patients who don't have insurance or cannot raise the expected amount upfront, when you know what really drove you to be a doctor is to save lives.

When you achieve financial freedom and money stops being the main motivator of what you do in life, you become free to make career choices that put your values at the forefront.

For example, as a doctor, you can join a non-profit organization that provides care for those patients who can't afford it.

2. It increases your sense of resilience

As you may have noticed by now, everyone in this life is faced by financial hardship at one point in life, whether that is a natural disaster like a hurricane that takes your house and everything in it away, a diagnosis like cancer that continuously makes you pay for expensive treatment or a financially draining divorce. These situations can make you go through a tough time financially.

One of the advantages of being financially free is that when all hell breaks loose financially, you can always use your savings or your rainy day fund to better deal with your financial hardship.

Here your savings will provide you with a glimpse of hope as you can use those savings to weather the storm.

For instance, if you lose a loved one, you can use your savings to cater for their burial and then follow that up with paying for therapy sessions, which will help you recover from the pain of losing your loved one or, in other words, help you to manage your grief.

In short, financial freedom helps increase your resilience.

3. It allows you to focus on what you want to do, not what you have to do

Another amazing benefit of being financially free is that it allows you to do what you want with your life and not what you have to do to survive.

Here is how.

Every human being, including you, has basic needs that you need to survive. You need food, shelter, and clothing, and you also need other things that make your life run smoothly like owning a car, being social, attending parties, going on vacations, and being charitable, among others. Then you have debts that are part of your needs because you need to pay them.

Now for you to fulfill all or most of those needs, you need a steady flow of income that can support your needs every month. When you haven't achieved financial freedom, your life normally revolves around you doing what you need to do to make those payments. This then makes you stuck in a job that you dislike or stuck working with clients that are not a good fit for you simply because you need to make ends meet.

When you become financially free, you don't worry about making payments, as your income is enough to cater for them anyway. This, in turn, enables you to do what you want in life, whether that is working in a job that you love or working with clients that fit your business. Basically, it gives you the ability to choose and enjoy what you love doing.

4. You get control over your time

One amazing thing that financial freedom gives you is the ability to use your time how you want it.

This is so because when all your expenses are covered, what you do with your time becomes up to you. You can decide to continue with your professional work for the love and passion for it or decide to quit your day job and pursue other interests like traveling or doing what you love, like singing or dancing.

Basically, financial freedom gives you the power to control your time.

5. *It allows you to be a risk-taker*

When you have financial freedom, your fear of being experimental with life is eliminated or drastically reduced and the world literally becomes your playground. It becomes easier for you to do things that you would have otherwise never have done but have always wanted to do them like, living in a different country, starting your own business, or launching your talent. And all that is because you were stuck in a job or business that you needed to be in to survive.

So when you achieve financial freedom, and you feel you are financially secure, you will have the ability to be a risk-taker, which will enable you to do some of the most daring things in life - and that's a good thing because that's what life is about, taking risks and discovering new things.

6. *You will have better health*

This might come as a shock to you, but financial freedom actually improves your health.

Take a minute and imagine you are living paycheck to paycheck, you have a huge amount of debt, and your boss has just announced that your company has been hit financially, and they will have to let some of the employees go.

How stressful is that?

Well, that is the life you live when you are not financially free. Your company might not face uncertainties, but you can't help it but be in a continuous mode of being worried about making ends meet. This increases the level of stress in your daily life. It limits your happiness, and because working takes almost all your time and leaves you with no time for you to do what you truly love, you end up living a miserable life, and your health takes a hit for it. Your lifestyle makes it easy for you to develop lifestyle diseases like diabetes, heart disease, hypertension, chronic fatigue, depression, and more.

As you now know, financial freedom gives you a sense of security, which enables you to do what you like without the pressure of bills and debts. This scenario enables you to do what you want in life, and some of these things are what help you improve your health.

Good examples include making time to exercise daily, preparing a healthy home-cooked meal, being able to have healthy working hours, and healthy sleeping time. You also get to have a great sense of emotional peace, which makes you happier and more content with your life. That is what greatly improves your health.

7. It increases your self-esteem

One of the best things that comes with you achieving financial freedom is you getting a sense of self accomplishment. You feel proud of yourself and you feel the progress you have just made has lifted your spirits and made you feel like you can do even bigger things.

Those feelings are what increases your self-esteem and your confidence and as you might know, increased self esteem turns you into a person who wants to improve different areas of your life including, your ability to reach your full potential in life and the quality of your relationship between you and your spouse or your family-which is a huge plus in your life.

8. *You will make your decisions based on your long term goals*

You might not know this but when your financial situation isn't great like when you are leaving from paycheck to pay check your decisions are usually based on short term goals or small goals. A good example is when you are paying mortgage or students loans-you will most often than not focus your mind on getting through the month, getting your paycheck and you making your monthly student loan payments.

While paying your debt is very important, you focusing your whole mind on paying your debt delays your progress in life and that's where financial freedom makes a huge difference in your life.

When you achieve financial freedom your decisions will start being based on your long term goals since your short term needs have been catered for whether that is food, shelter, debt or clothing. You will find yourself comfortably thinking about where you want to be in 10 years and what are the steps that you will need to take to get there.

In summary, financial freedom helps you become more progressive in your thinking which automatically helps you make more wealth and boost your financial freedom.

As you have just seen, achieving financial freedom is a huge boost for your life, which makes you wonder - why is financial freedom such a rare occurrence? Why don't you hear of it a lot? Well, the answer to that question lies in the chapter below.

WHY IS FINANCIAL FREEDOM SO ELUSIVE?

As you have just seen, achieving financial freedom is one of the best things you can do in life. With it, you will live a financially fearless life where you can just concentrate on doing what you love instead of doing what can earn you 'survival money.'

This might make you wonder:

Why are you not financially free right now?

I mean, we all would love to be financially free based on the reasons we discussed earlier...

It's a good thing right? Then why haven't you ever worked towards it?

Here is why:

While you may desire to reach financial freedom or reach a place where you have no debts and don't have to worry too much about making money because you have enough investments and passive income businesses to take care of that, there are a couple of psychological, cultural and social reasons that stand in your way. These reasons make you struggle with money and financial responsibilities-almost the same way you struggle with eating healthy.

Before you can learn how to build wealth and achieve financial freedom, it is important for you to first understand those reasons that have made you a slave to money (for lack of better word). This is important because by highlighting these reasons, you can unravel the reason why you are where you are financially, and once you do, it will become easier for you to change your mentality and adopt a new mindset that supports healthy habits around money.

Here are the top 5 reasons you fail when it comes to taking control of your finances and cultivating financial freedom.

1. Restrictive beliefs about money

You may not have realized it, but everyone has some ingrained beliefs about money. These beliefs (if they are negative) may limit your ability to create wealth and be financially free. These types of beliefs run deep because they come from the personal experiences you have had in life, your social conventions, and the culture you grew up in.

These beliefs hinder your ability to create wealth because they create what is called an "upper money limit" in your mind. The "upper money limit" is an amount of income that you are comfortable with. So once you reach that limit, you unconsciously lose motivation to go past that limit.

Here are the common limiting beliefs and how you can conquer them and have a positive money mindset.

– Money is the root of all evil

This is one of the cultural beliefs that stand in your way of making money. The idea that money is the root of all evil comes from the Bible and, more specifically, from 1st Timothy 6:10.

If you turn on the news today, you won't miss stories of corruption from different governments in the world, stories about evils that dishonest Fortune 500 CEOs or bank executives are doing, and generally just stories of how the 'rich' are behaving badly.

But does this really make money inherently evil?

The answer is no. Yes, it shows some truths in the belief that money is evil, but money in itself isn't evil. However, greedy and corrupt people do evil things with it.

To overcome this belief, you don't have to change the belief that money is evil because, as you saw above, it can be evil. What you need to change is your orientation toward the belief. You can do so by defining what money is to you.

For instance, you can say something like *"money is an abundant resource that will help me do well in life and the lives of others"*. Basically, refute the belief that money is evil to you by telling yourself the positives that money will bring to your life.

- *Money doesn't buy happiness*

Another limiting belief is that money cannot buy you happiness.

The idea behind this belief is that wealth makes you live a miserable life. It implies that when you become wealthy, you separate yourself from the people that you love (family and friends) as you will most often than not, move out of your neighborhood and change your lifestyle to mirror your new environment, which automatically separates you from the life that you were living before the money.

This might surprise you, but this belief is actually correct; money can't buy you happiness. This is because happiness is a feeling that comes from doing what you love, having good people in your life, and you spending your time in pursuits that add value to your life.

That said, the misleading thing about this belief is how it connects wealth to unhappiness, creating a perception that wealth creation is the source of unhappiness when it's not.

Wealth does not promote unhappiness. In fact, what it does is that it helps you create the feelings of happiness in your life through buying the resources you need to be happy, whether that is a plane ticket to see your favorite city in Europe or a house you need to take care of homeless kids, which is what you love doing.

In short, unhappiness is not a direct result of wealth creation. The two are not connected. So change your perception of seeing money as a source of unhappiness and just concentrate on how money can help you do the things that make you happy.

- *It takes money to make money*

This is another perception that may hinder you from launching a new business, funding an investment, or having a side hustle that will help you achieve financial freedom. If you have this belief, you believe that for you to create a successful business or make a profitable investment somewhere, you need a specific amount of money in your bank, or you won't succeed. Now since you don't have this amount of money, you shy away from doing something extra in your life.

So how do you deal with this belief?

The truth is; there is always a certain amount of money that you will be required to have for you to invest or run a business. That said, money is not the most important thing when it comes to investing or doing a business.

Having a brilliant idea and a great strategy is.

So it's not a must that you have $100,000 in your bank to start a business; you can find a profitable business that only needs $1,000 or less to start. And even though its profits won't be as huge as the $100,000 one, they will still be profits you can use to build your business to a profit that helps you achieve financial freedom.

– *I have zero control over whether I become wealthy*

This belief, which is one of the most damaging beliefs that may stand in your way of making wealth and being financially free, is a belief you tend to grow up with as you watch your parents work hard every day to earn money. Then when you grow older and start working and earning money yourself, the belief grows further in you because you feel your income and how much you make is fully dependant on other people like your boss who sets your salary, or a client who chooses whether or not to give you their business.

This belief makes you feel like becoming wealthy is someone else's choice and that you have no control over it. As a result, you get blinded by the perception that you have no control over your wealth creation, so you can't plan or take action that leads to you being wealthy and financially free because the ending doesn't rest with you.

How do you deal with this belief?

To deal with this belief, you will first need to convince yourself that you are in control of the process of building wealth in your life. To do that, you will need to look at stories of people who have managed to take control of their financial situations and worked their way into building immense amounts of wealth. Such people include Elon Musk-the CEO of Space X & Tesla, Richard Brandson-founder of the Virgin Group, J.K Rowling-author of the Harry Potter series, Robert Kiyosaki-author of Rich Dad Poor Dad, and Jimmy Carey –the famous Hollywood actor, among others.

That step will inspire you and help eliminate the belief that you have no control over your wealth creation process. After that, you will need to sit down with yourself and figure out what lifestyle you want to live and how much wealth you need to create and then start figuring out how to make all that happen. Don't worry too much about making it happen right now because this book will, later on, show you the ways you can use to achieve financial freedom. In short, focus on the idea of making good money than the money needed.

2. *Believing that financial freedom is impossible for you*

Financial independence is a great thing. You stop worrying about covering your basic needs; you are free to travel wherever and whenever you want, and you can buy anything you want without feeling guilty. Pretty great, ha!

One of the things that has been hindering you from achieving financial freedom is your belief that financial freedom is impossible for you. Every time you think of how nice your life could be when you're financially free, a small voice from deep inside, you tells you to stop dreaming. It tells you financial freedom is too good to be true and that you will never achieve it. That small voice does not only kill your belief in financial abundance but also stops you from taking actions that would lead you to financial freedom.

What you should do to combat this hindrance is learning how financial freedom is achieved and what it takes for you to achieve it. You can learn that by reading books about finance, interviewing people who are financially free, and getting to know how they did it or attending financial seminars. This will help you understand the roadmap to financial freedom and help you understand everyone, including you, can be financially free and that all you need is to follow some steps.

3. *The psychology of scarcity*

The other reason why it has been hard for you to achieve financial freedom is because of the psychology of scarcity. The psychology of scarcity is a mindset that you adopt when you feel like you have or make too little.

Here is how it works.

When you feel like what you are earning in life is too little, you automatically develop a mindset of focusing all your attention on what you don't have. Now since your focus is very powerful, what happens is; you will focus on one thing and neglect other things of value, and this is what happens when you are poor, or you don't make enough. Every month you focus your attention on paying bills and paying your loans, and you neglect the thought of saving to better your future.

To overcome the psychology of scarcity, you need to sit down and write down your goals. Break them down into short term goals that are manageable. This will help you to stop focusing only on managing your financial scarcity and see important things like working towards financial freedom.

4. *The lack of financial education*

One of the huge barriers to financial freedom is the lack of financial education.

For years now, graduates, including those who major in economics, finance, accounting and business-related professions, have gone to get good jobs but still end up in huge debts and having no investments.

So how is this possible?

This is possible because there is nothing in your formal education system that taught you about personal finance. No one taught you how to think about money, lessons of investing, tax strategies, or having a wealth mindset, which are all critical topics for you as an adult. And your culture isn't different either as a majority of the cultures around the world avoid the money talk-so much so that financial literacy has become a global problem.

The impact of financial illiteracy is what has led to money relations strategies that make it extremely hard for you to achieve financial freedom.

One such strategy is where you play the "let me accumulate as much money as possible" game so that you can be financially secure-without you knowing that accumulating money makes you a slave to money and that you can also never be financial free with that method because your security will only last as long as you are working. The right way to go about it is you focusing your energy on accumulating assets, which can earn you passive income, as this would mean you have money working for you.

To change this situation, you need to invest in financial education. Start by attending financial seminars and compliment that with reading financial books and courses.

Some of the best books include;

- Rich Dad Poor Dad
- Think and Grow Rich
- The Millionaire next door, among others

5. *The lack of patience and commitment*

One of the most common reasons why you are where you are financially and why its extremely hard for you to achieve financial freedom is because you lack patience and commitment.

JK Rowling, the author of the Harry Potter series and maybe the world's richest author in the world, spent years (with some saying more than 5 years) writing her first book, *Harry Potter and the Philosopher's Stone.* During that time, she relied on the money she got from the welfare benefit to survive with her daughter. After she was done with her book, she took it for publishing, where it got rejected by a dozen publishers before it later got published in the US and became a worldwide phenomenon.

The JK Rowling story is the perfect example of how creating wealth and achieving financial freedom works. Financial freedom is usually a journey that does not happen overnight or in a few years. For you to achieve it, it will take you 4-5 or even more than 6 years and those are years where you are fully committed to your goal the same way JK Rowling was committed to writing her book despite her challenging circumstances.

The one reason why you may not have achieved financial freedom could be because you lack the patience to commit to a formula that can help you achieve financial freedom. You live in an instant satisfaction society where you are constantly influenced to spend or consume your money for a self-gratification feeling, which makes it hard for you to sacrifice your present fulfillment urges and take years to build yourself a financially free life.

For you to achieve financial freedom, you will need to adopt the abundance mindset that helps you focus on what you can produce for yourself rather than what you can consume. You also need to convince yourself that patience pays and that it will require sacrifice for you to be financially free.

Now that you know how advantageous financial freedom is and you have learned what has been standing on your way to achieving financial freedom, now is time for you to learn the simple path you can use to achieve financial freedom.

A SIMPLE PATH TO BUILDING WEALTH

The truth of the matter is building wealth has always been a simple thing to do. It might seem hard for you because you don't know the proven formula to wealth creation.

But not to worry because that is what this chapter is going to teach you.

What you are about to learn in this chapter is timeless wisdom that has been used by multitudes of successful people out there and has been proven to work and can also work for you.

This proven formula, which is also the missing ingredient that you have been missing to yield breakthrough results in wealth creation, is better explained in three parts that need to be followed simultaneously.

Here are the three parts that will give you a step by step formulae to financial freedom.

PART 1: Preparing Yourself For Financial Freedom

(i) Cultivate a positive mindset about money

Jen Sincero, in his book, '*You Are a Badass at Making Money*', says if you are a person who doesn't make a lot of money, most often than not you, will feel shame when it comes to you making more money. You will feel guilty for having the money and guiltier for wanting to make more money. And just like the factors you saw in the previous chapter, those feelings are what turn to be your greatest obstacles when it comes to making money.

So for you to experience financial freedom, you will first need to change your mindset towards money. You will need to stop seeing money as a bad thing or an evil thing and start seeing it for what it truly is, an essential need in your life.

Money is what you use to buy your basic needs like food, clothing, and shelter. Money is also the device that helps you live the life you want and helps you achieve your dreams, whether that is living in a big house or buying a large acre of land for farming.

What you have just learned is what you need to tell yourself every day to eradicate any negative views you might have about money because those views subconsciously damage your chances of making money and keeping it.

So write down at least ten things that money can do to your life that are positive and read them out twice a day. This will help change your negative mentality about money.

(ii) Write down your financial goals

Why do you need to achieve financial freedom? What are you looking to accomplish?

Do you want to be able to quit your 8 to 5 job finally? Are you desperate to get rid of your student loan? Have you always wanted to travel the world and need a stable income flow to do that? Do you want to have enough money to buy your dream car or house? Or perhaps you want to start your own business?

To achieve financial freedom, you need to have a 'why you are doing it'. It needs to be a strong why, and this is because when you know why you are doing something, you tend to be more motivated to do it.

The questions you have just seen are some of the questions that you need to ask yourself to find out why you want to achieve financial freedom- and it is okay for you to have multiple reasons why you are doing them.

Once you find out your why, you now need to write down your goal.

For instance, if you want to pay your student loan, buy a house and start your own business, you can write down:

I want to;

- Pay off $40,000 worth of students loan
- Save $30,000 to use as a down payment for my house
- Make $150,000 selling my hair products online.

Basically, set your financial goals and place them where you can be able to view them daily. Then form a habit of taking 5-7 minutes every day to view and visualize your goals coming true. You can do this early in the morning before you get out of your room or do it as the first order of business when you get to work. This will help you attract your goals, which will increase your chances of accomplishing them.

PART 2: Manage Your Finances

(i) Be aware of your starting point

To achieve financial freedom, you need to manage your finances. For you to do that, you will need first to know where you stand financially. In short, you need to evaluate yourself and see what your financial situation looks like.

- **The first thing you will need to do is to write down** your monthly income. This is any income you get in a month, including your salary, money from an investment, or money from a side hustle that you have. Write your total income down and set it aside.

- Next, **you will need to record your expenses** or, in other words, track your monthly spending. Make a list of how you spend your money each month. Look at the money you spend for food, for rent, for clothes, for going out on dates, for entertainment, and just about everything else that you spend your money on and come up with a total amount of your expense.

- **The next step is for you to take account of how much debt you have.** Create a list of all your debts, including credit cards, car loans, student loans, mortgages, money owed to friends and family, and any other debt you might have. Do not despair if you have a huge debt; this book will teach you how to pay that debt down later.

- **Next, take account of all the money you have saved.** Make a list of all savings, including the company retirement program, stocks, and money in your savings account. Take that number and set it aside.

This step will most probably serve you with a depressing reality of your financial situation, but it is an important step for you to take.

For the sake of better understanding, let's say after all those exercises, you found out the following.

- Your monthly income, which is composed of the only salary, is $5,000
- Your monthly expenses amount to $3,500.
- Your total saving is only $300
- Your total debt is $300,000

Take a close look at those numbers. You will notice one important thing: if the numbers above represented your current situation, you would be living from hand to mouth or living from paycheck to paycheck.

This is because, according to the example, the money you are left with after you subtract your expenses from your income is $1,500. You haven't even paid your monthly debt yet, which means that amount could go lower or amount to zero, depending on your monthly debt payment.

There is a huge possibility that your situation is no different from the one you have just seen, but you shouldn't be worried because the next step below will teach you how to regain the health of your finances.

(ii) Make more than you spend

Now that you have taken a look at your financial situation and probably seen how bad it is, the next step is to improve your financial situation.

As you will come to see in part three, achieving financial freedom requires you to have a bit of extra money after you have taken care of all your expenses. This extra money is what you will use to build wealth, as you will come to see, which is why it's essential for you to change your financial situation to one that leaves you with a good amount of money to spare after you subtract your expenses from your income.

Now there are two ways you can do it.

- You can start by cutting down your expenses to save a bit of money
- The other one is increasing your income by making more money

Here is an explanation of the two methods.

– *Cut down your spending*

Mike Tyson, who is one of the top heavyweight boxers to ever box, went from having $300 million in his bank account to being in debt in 10 years. His mistake? His spending. It is alleged that Mike Tyson used to spend $400,000 each month.

Another good example of spending is one of Warren Buffet and Kanye West. In 1958, one of the richest men on earth, Warren Buffet, bought a five-bedroom house worth $31,500, and he lives in that house up to date despite him being worth over $90 billion. On the other side, Kanye West whose net worth is less than a billion, lives in a $20 million house, and at one point in Kanye's life, he found himself in a $53 million debt. This perfectly shows what really separates a financially successful person from a financially unsuccessful person- their spending.

Warren Buffet is successful because he doesn't spend more than he needs to while Kanye ended up in a debt for spending money he doesn't have, which is the same thing that happened to Mike Tyson.

So what you need to learn is how to spend money like a financially successful person. And it is simple really-only spend money on what is necessary for your life and minimize expenses where you can.

For instance:

- If you have rent a three-bedroom house and live alone, shift to a cheaper one-bedroom house.
- If you drive to work and back every day, you can reduce your cost of gas by joining your area's car-pool society.
- If you spend a lot on clothes, cut your budget in half because financial freedom is way more fulfilling to achieve than a fashionable look. Besides, Zuckerberg, who is a billionaire, wears the same style of boring jeans and a t-shirt every day.
- Reduce your budget for eating out.
- If a lot of your money goes to partying, reduce partying to one or twice in a month.

When you cut back your spending, one thing works in your favor, and that is you get more money to put aside for financial freedom. What you need to do now is to go through your expense list and start doing away with things that you can live perfectly without as well as reducing your expenses where you can.

— Make more money

The second thing you can do to improve the money you put aside after expenses is for you to figure out a way of making more money i.e. increase your income.

How do you do that?

Well, there are a couple of strategies you can use to make more money.

- One is you finding a side hustle. The best side hustle is the one that is connected to what you are doing.

For instance, if you are an engineer, you can offer consultation services on the weekends as your side hustle. If you work for a studio as a cameraman, you can start taking photos as your side hustle. But this is not to say you can't start a side hustle that is unrelated to your career.

- Secondly, you can ask for a raise in your company or work for more hours to earn more money.
- Thirdly you can change jobs to go to a company that pays you more.

The main idea of making more than you spend is to make sure the gap between what you earn and what you spend is big enough for you to have a good amount of money as the difference to use to build your wealth.

When you combine cutting down your spending with raising your income, you will surely have a good amount of money that you can use to build wealth.

With all that in mind, let's move to part three, which is where you learn how to build wealth. In short, it helps you create a positive cash flow that you use to invest and produce another positive cash flow.

PART 3: Wealth Creation

(i) Invest wisely

Now that you have created a positive cash flow, it is time for you to create wealth, and the first thing you are going to do is to invest wisely.

What investing wisely will do for you is that it will create another positive cash flow, other than your current cash flow, which is what will help you reach financial freedom.

When it comes down to it, financial freedom is achieved by making smart investments. This entails you placing your money in an investment vehicle that earns you a good interest rate or gives you a good return rate that ends up building you enough wealth over a long period for you to be free financially.

The best investment for you to make are the ones that provide you with passive income. Passive income is an earning that is derived from a business in which you are not actively involved in.

Investing in passive income is wise because you do not trade your time for money as you do in your job. Here you just make an investment, and you sit back and let your money work for you.

"If you want to become really wealthy, you must have your money work for you" John D. Rockefeller.

So what are the best passive income investments for you to make?

Before you take a look at some of the best investment vehicles that can earn you passive income, you need to know the pay **yourself first** concept.

Pay Yourself First

The **pay yourself first** concept is one of the secrets to making wealth. This concept tells you to take a specific amount of your income (preferably 10%) as soon as you get paid and set it aside for investing. This means the first thing you will need to do with your $5,000 income, according to the example, is to set aside $500 every month for investing. That is the money you will use to invest wisely.

"Wealth beyond your wildest dreams is possible if you follow the golden rule: Invest ten percent of all you make for long-term growth"
- David Chilton, The Wealthy Barber.

Now that you know where your investment money is coming from, it's time for you to look at the investment vehicles that will help you achieve financial freedom.

Here they are.

1. Stocks

One way you can use to build long-term wealth and income that eventually helps you become financially free is by investing in stocks.

Stocks are basically equity investments that symbolize legal ownership in a company. When you buy a stock, you usually own a part of that company.

There are two ways you make money from stocks.

- Through you getting dividend payments
- Through the price appreciation of the stock, which essentially means you can cash the gains by selling your stock

For example, if you put down an initial investment of $2,000 in stock and each month you invest an addition $200 for 20 years, earning a 10% return, at the end of 20 years, you will end up with $150,915 when you only contributed $50,000.

But why invest in stocks?

One of the things that makes stocks such a good investment vehicle is that stocks always go up over time. That is why stocks are one of the best performing investment vehicles over time.

Now the best stocks for you to invest in are stocks funds. This is because with them, you don't need to get involved with analyzing stocks; they do it for you, and all that you are left with is to just sit down and watch your money work for you. Besides, this is a simple path to wealth book, not a hardworking path to wealth.

I will give you an example of one of the biggest stock funds in the US.

VTSAX (Vanguard Total Stock Market)

VTSAX is the largest mutual fund supplier in the US right now. The fund is designed to cover virtually all investible stocks. The fund's top holdings are in Johnson and Johnson, Facebook, Amazon.com, Microsoft, and Apple.

The minimum investment that you will be required to have to invest in VTSAX is $3,000. You will have an expense ratio of 0.04%-which is amazing because it means you will be paying $4 each year for management expenses.

VTSAX is perfect for you because it has a high annual return rate that can really propel you into financial freedom. For instance, if you invested $10,000 in VTSAX in 2001, your shares will today be worth about $35,000.

All you need to do now is to visit Vanguard.

https://investor.vanguard.com/corporate-portal/

You can set up a free account and start investing. However, there are many others out there. This is not an endorsement for the mutual fund but is meant to be an example.

2. *Bonds*

As good as stocks are, it is always good for you to mix them up with bonds. This is because bonds are more steady and reliable than stocks, and so they can help you smoothen out any bumpy rides you might get from your stock investments.

A bond is an amount of money that you lend to a company or the government for a specific period, mostly between 6 months to 30 years, and in return, the company or the government pays you back your investment, plus interest once the bond reaches its maturity date.

For example, you can buy a 10 year, $15,000 bond paying 5% interest. This bond will pay you 5% of $15,000 every six months and then give you back your $15,000 after the 10 years. It is an amazing way of accumulating wealth and making your money work for you.

As a person who is not yet wealthy and cannot come up with $10,000 or $15,000 at once, the best thing for you to do is to invest in bonds through bond funds. Bond funds basically take money from multiple investors and put it in a pool. A fund manager then uses that money to invest in high-interest individual bonds, and the interest is trickled down to the investors.

Here are some of the top bond funds you can invest in.

– NEFRX (Loomis Sayles Core Plus Bond Fund)

This refund requires a minimum investment of $2,500. Bonds in this fund have an average maturity of 9.01 years. This fund provides you with high total returns but also carries with it a higher level of risk than most funds because it deals with fixed-income securities, which are high yielding but risky. It has a slightly high expense ratio of 0.73%.

- **MWTRX (Metropolitan West Total Return Bond Fund)**

The MWTRX invests in a wide range of fixed-income securities. It requires you to make an initial investment of $5,000. Its expense ratio is 0.67% and its average maturity period is 7.69 years.

- **VTBM (Vanguard Total Bond Market)**

VTBM is one of the best bonds you can invest in.

This is because:

- It doesn't have a minimum initial investment requirement
- It has a very low expense ratio of 0.035%, nice ha!

The fund mostly invests in government bonds, and its average duration of maturity is 6.5 years.

- **DODIX (Dodge and Cox Income Fund)**

DODIX fund invests in investment-grade securities, and it requires you to have an initial investment of $2,500. It also has a very low expense ratio of 0.42%.

Those are some of the bond funds you can invest in. Check them out and choose the one that suits you the best.

3. Real Estate

Another great investment vehicle you can use to build wealth long term is investing in real estate.

Investing in real estate used to be a huge hustle in the past because it needed you to have huge amounts of money, time, and expertise. But thanks to real estate investing apps, today you can invest in high yielding real estate properties with a reasonable amount of money.

Here are now some of the best real estate investing apps you can consider investing in.

– RealtyMogul

Realty Mogul is a crowdfunding platform that pulls together money from investors and use it to purchase large ticket properties like retail space and office buildings. To invest in this app, you will need a minimum investment of $5,000.

- Roofstock

This app deals with selling family homes that may or may not have been rehabbed. It is one of the best real estate investment apps, and you should check it out.

- Fund Rise

This investing app specializes in real estate investment trusts REITs.

So if you don't have the time to manage a property, REITs are for you. REITs manage income-producing properties for you and then distribute the profit down to you as an investor.

Investing in REITs used to be very expensive in the past, but through Fund Rise, you can invest in REITs, and you only need a minimum investment of $500.

The simple path to wealth requires you to use simple yet effective ways of building your wealth, and that is what the three methods of investing you have just learned will help you do.

4. *High yielding savings accounts*

A high-yield savings account is another financial investment vehicle that you can use to make your money work for you and help you achieve financial freedom.

But what really is a high-yield saving account?

It is a type of savings account that you can deposit your money into and generally earn a greater interest rate on your deposits than you would have earned with a traditional savings account.

Traditional savings accounts from most traditional brick and mortar banks will mostly give you a 0.01%-0.10% interest rate (known as APY – annual percentage yield). On the other side, a high-yielding savings account will give you an interest rate that ranges from 0.4%-0.9%- which is huge. Online banks offer the highest rates for high-yield savings accounts.

To show you how huge that is, let's assume you have a balance of $10,000 after one year, with no additional deposit in a traditional savings account that has 0.01% interest rate, and in a high yield savings account that has an interest rate of 0.9%. Assume all are compounded monthly.

At the end of that year, your balance in the traditional savings account will be $10,001, and the one in your high-yield saving account will be $10,090.37. An income difference of $90.37.

In short, a high yield savings account means you are getting a better return on your money, which is what you need to be financially free. You earn 90 times more based on our example.

You now must be wondering; how do you find the best high-yielding savings account? Well, there are numerous high yield savings accounts out there, and they are all different, with some having higher interest rates than others, some having minimum monthly balance requirements while others don't and some having maintenance and other associated fees while others don't. The trick to coming up with the best high yield saving account is reading all the fine print to find an account that has a high-interest rate and, at the same time, has low fees. I mentioned earlier that online banks tend to have better rates than traditional, brick and mortar banks.

To help you with that decision, here is a list of some of the best high yielding savings accounts.

- **CIT Bank** has an interest rate of 0.5%.
- **PenFed** has an interest rate of 0.6%
- **MySavings** has an interest rate of 0.7%
- **Axos** has an interest rate of 0.6%

You can also refer to this extended resource for more ideas:

https://www.nerdwallet.com/best/banking/high-yield-online-savings-accounts

One of the reasons why high yield savings accounts are ideal is because they are mostly insured by the government, which makes them less risky and a good place for you to invest cash that you will need in the future.

5. Annuities

Another great source of passive income that can help you live a financially free life, especially after retirement, is annuities.

Annuities are insurance contracts that provide you with a future income stream or a lump-sum payment. To invest in an annuity product, you will need to pay a single upfront payment or make a series of small amounts of payments to the insurance company. During your retirement, the insurance company will send you a lump sum payment or send you multiple payments.

Upon maturity, the payouts you will receive in this investment depend on the type of annuity you choose and the details of that annuity. Basically, there are three types of annuities:

– *Fixed annuities*

In a fixed annuity, the insurance company offers you a set rate of interest that is not tied to or affected by market rates. The interest rate is locked and gives you that sense of security of knowing exactly what you will get from your investment.

– *Variable annuities*

A variable annuity is an opposite of what a fixed annuity is. This is because the amount you will receive in the future, when you choose a variable annuity will be based on the amount you put down, the return of the investment you choose in your annuity, and other expenses or fees that the annuity will charge. This type of annuity can help you get higher payouts, but it can also result in a low payout rate.

– *Indexed annuities*

An indexed annuity is a combination of a fixed and variable annuity. In this type of annuity, your investment can get protection from drops in the market. That said, you cannot benefit as much as you could in the variable annuity when the market does well.

To get started, buy an annuity straight from an insurance company. You can also buy one from financial groups, banks, and independent brokers. Some of the annuity companies you can consider include;

- Fidelity annuities

- Facet wealth
- AgeUp
- Annuity Gator
- Blueprint income

6. *Building CD ladder*

A CD or a certificate of deposit is one of the best low-risk tools you can use to make passive income that will help you become financially free. Building a CD ladder is an investment strategy that involves buying a series of individual certificates of deposits from banks with different maturity dates that enable you to build up your interest over a specific period.

Are you confused?

Let me break it down for you. Certificates of deposit have different maturity dates starting from a 6 months maturity date all the way up to 5 years maturity date. The longer the maturity date, the more interest your invested money will gain.

Here is an example of how CD rates rise over a long period of time.

- 1 year CD- 2.50%|
- 2 year CD- 2.90%
- 3 year CD- 3.05%
- 4 year CD- 3.10%
- 5 year CD- 3.15%

How do you build a CD ladder?

To build a CD ladder, you need to open multiple CDs with various maturity dates. As soon as the first one matures, you reinvest the amount in another CD with a longer maturity period to earn you more interest.

So let's say you want to build a 4 year CD ladder and you have $6,000 to invest. You will divide the money equally into four CDs with post apart maturity dates.

- $1,500 into 1 year CD with 2.5%APY
- $1,500 into 2 year CD with 2.9%APY
- $1,500 into 3 year CD with 3.05%APY
- $1,500 into 4 year CD with 3.1%APY

One year after the investment, the first CD will mature. When that happens, you will reinvest that money into a certificate of deposit that offers a greater yield than the one year one. When the second CD matures, you will do the same and reinvest it in another CD that offers higher yields than the 2 year CD. Do the same for the 3 year CD. Continue reinvesting the maturing CD to a higher-yielding CD. This can be you reinvesting any CD that matures with buying a new four year CD.

Now the length on the CD ladder will depend on your goals. If, for instance, you want to achieve financial freedom after 15 years, you can build the ladder and reinvest for 15 years.

This is a perfect way for you to build a good amount of passive income.

7. *Listing your property on Airbnb*

Another amazing way that you can use to make passive income and build wealth that will help you achieve financial freedom is by you listing your property on a vacation rental site like Airbnb, Vrbo, Booking.com or TripAdvisor and start earning money from bookings.

This type of investment is for if you own a house or an apartment that you don't live in or you hardly use or one that has extra room. That said, listing your property will first require you to do some work or get involved in the business because you will need to work on preparing your place, listing it, and marketing it. After that, the business can become passive, but you will have to hire a property manager that will deal with the day-to-day work involving your property like collecting rent, cleaning up after guests, and fixing the place up.

In 2018, the director of public affairs at Airbnb, Nick Papas, said an average Airbnb host could make about $7,200 in a year. As you can see, this type of investment can help you build wealth.

8. Creating A Course

If you are highly knowledgeable in a particular subject matter, you can create a passive income stream that will help you achieve financial freedom by simply listing it on some of the popular marketplaces for online courses, like Udemy.

Let me break it down for you.

Udemy is an online platform with numerous video courses that teach a wide range of subjects. Users pay to access the course materials for whatever they want to learn.

Now when you are highly knowledgable on lets say what you do at work which can be, an accountant, a music producer, a lawyer, a chef or a gym instructor, you can use that knowledge to create a complete video course and allow users to purchase it on a platform like Udemy.

The good thing about selling a course on Udemy is you will only be required to work initially, but once your course is on Udemy, you could afford to sit back and wait for sales to come in, especially if you created a course that gives students value, as they are likely to leave positive feedback, which would, in turn, make your course more popular.

A course on Udemy is priced between $20 and $200. This means you can easily make $1,000 annually or even more, and all you need is to sell your courses to over 20 people per year on an average of $50.

Tip: If you can commit to updating your course regularly, you could structure your course as a subscription product so that you have students sticking to the course over the course of several months or years to keep getting value from your lessons.

9. Self-publishing books

One of the smartest ways you can use to create wealth and become financially free is through self-publishing books online.

In the first six months of 2020, eBooks sales were up 12.7%, which come in at $544.5 million. This statistic shows you three important things.

- People still love reading.
- A huge number of people who read go for eBooks
- Last but not least and perhaps the most important point, is that the eBook industry is a huge industry that you can take advantage of and build yourself wealth that can help you become financially free.

So if you have always been a good writer or are extremely knowledgable on a particular subject, you can do what is called self-publishing, which is incredibly easy. All you need to do is to write a book, edit the book, create an attractive cover for it and then upload it on a platform like

Amazon's Kindle Direct Publishing. When the book is live, you will start earning passive income from your book sales.

If you are not talented when it comes to writing or are too busy, you can hire the services of a ghostwriter who can write a book for you at a fee. After that, you can publish the book as your own (the ghostwriter transfers all copyrights to the book upon completion of the project.

That said, don't expect immediate success when you go into selling e-books. This is because for this vehicle to turn into a powerful passive income vehicle, it will take some time and marketing, but the potential is huge.

The self-publishing space is a numbers game – unless you have a big name or following, you cannot afford to publish just one book.

Think of it this way; if you can make just $30 per month from a single book that you paid a ghostwriter to write for $200, in 12 months, the book will have generated $360. Now imagine having 10 books or even more, and you are looking at well over $3,000 in a year.

As you learn the ropes of self-publishing, you learn what topics sell better, how to do keyword research, cover creation, and much more. All that will prove very helpful, as you may probably end up creating a book that can generate several hundred dollars or even several thousand dollars a month.

Tip: You can fast track the process of perfecting your self-publishing skillset by enrolling to a self-publishing course. The investment for enrolling to the course is likely to be a drop in the ocean compared to how much you stand to gain in terms of potential earnings. What's more – there are free courses on YouTube.

You can hire ghostwriters on places like Fiverr, Upwork and ghostwriting companies.

Other ways you can make extra money, although a little more involving to build, include:

- Building a blog and monetizing it using affiliate marketing, having membership sections, offering advertising space, selling your own products, etc.
- Selling (dropshipping) physical products on your own website, Shopify, eBay, Etsy, Amazon, and other platforms
- Creating and selling software, themes, and other digital products that you charge either a flat fee or an ongoing fee
- And much more

(ii) Set up an emergency fund

As you invest in the wealth creation vehicles, you will need an emergency fund. This fund will help you cater for any emergency that might arise in your life, something that will stop you from reaching out for your credit card and spending money that you don't have or you interrupting your debt payment or investment plan to cover for an emergency.

A good amount to save in your emergency account is $1,000-$5,000. So sacrifice a month or two of investing and come up with an emergency account. Financial experts recommend that it is necessary to have 3-6 months' worth of living expenses in your emergency fund.

That said, the money should only be used for emergencies like a leaking roof, a car breakdown or a hospital bill and not for financing a birthday party or taking your family out to eat, which are all things you can survive without.

(iii) Have a retirement fund

Now that your emergency fund is active and has been tucked in, the next step is for you to start contributing towards a retirement fund, with the most popular one being the 401k.

Typically, your employer matches your 401k contributions but up to a certain level. For instance, an employer can match 50% of the first 3% of contributions. If they do that, make sure to contribute 3%. If they match at 5% then contribute 5%. This is a nice way of you taking advantage of the free money that your employer is offering you.

401k is very important when it comes to building your wealth. This is because it helps you come up with a retirement plan that can help you become financially free and help you retire early.

For example, suppose you start saving $250 every month in your 401k fund at age 25. In that case, it is estimated that you can hit a million dollars by the time you are 65 years (40 years later), which is an amazingly huge amount of money. But the good thing about this example is it shows you can also decide to save for 20 years instead of 40, retire early at the age of 45 years and approximately get out with $500,000, which is also a good amount of money.

Start contributing to your 401k in a percentage that matches your employer's contribution and then increase that percentage as your monthly expense load is reduced, especially after clearing your debts.

(iv) Pay your debt

Now that you have an emergency account and you are matching your employer's 401k contribution, it's time for you to focus on clearing your debt.

For you to achieve financial freedom, you need to be debt-free. So as you continue investing, you should also focus on paying off your debts.

You now must be wondering how is paying your debt a step to wealth creation. Here is how; when you pay all your debts, it means each month from the day that you become debt-free you will be $1,000, $2,000, or even $5,000 richer, depending on the amount of money you have been using each month to pay your debt. And that brings you closer to financial freedom.

Now when it comes down to it, there are two methods that you can use to pay off your debt.

1. *Snowball method*

This method asks you to pay the smallest debt that you have first.

Let's assume your loan is;

- **Student loan- $60,000**
- **Credit card loan- $3,500**
- **Mortgage loan- $180,000**
- **Friend's loan- $20,000**

When you use this method, you will be required to first focus all your attention on paying your credit card loan, which means you will pay the minimum loan amount for the other loans that you have and then concentrate all the money that has been left on paying the credit card loan. Once you are through with the credit card loan, go for your friend's loan and so forth.

This method helps you clear out small loans fast, which helps you get motivated and encouraged to tackle the much bigger loans.

2. *Avalanche method*

This method asks you first to pay the debt with the highest interest rate.

Let's assume the list below represents the debt you have - ranked by how high the interest rate is, with number one having the highest interest rate and number last having the least interest rate.

- **Mortgage loan**
- **Student loan**
- **Credit card loan**
- **Friends loan**

So here, you will concentrate on paying your mortgage loan first and then focus on the next loan that has the second-highest interest loan. This method helps you lift a massive weight on your shoulder when you clear the highest interest rate loan that you have. The fact that you have cleared such a huge loan also motivates you to clear the lesser loans remaining.

Look at both methods and see what works best for you and use it to clear your debt.

(v) Increase your investment, emergency savings and retirement savings.

Once you have paid all your debts, the amount of your savings will greatly increase.

The last step is for you to actually use that saving to improve your investments, your emergency fund, and your retirement savings.

You can start by concentrating on increasing your emergency fund savings to 3-6 months' worth of your expenses. This will automatically improve your financial security. You will be in a position where you can survive for six months without an income.

You can then increase your retirement savings to up to 15% or an even higher amount.

Lastly, you can increase the amount of money you invest, which will help you build wealth at an even faster rate.

CONCLUSION

Financial freedom might seem challenging, especially if you feel you don't make a lot of money and are neck-deep in debt. However, what you might not know is you can still achieve it even with those challenges. All you need to do is change your financial practices and mirror the financial practices explained to you in this guide.

Stick to these newly developed financial practices and be consistent, and you will soon achieve financial freedom.

9 798593 137937